DUH!! It's Just Stocks

The Basics of the Stock Market

BY: S. Marie

Table of Contents

Introduction

Have you ever wanted to know something like a different language or how to breakdance but no matter what you did you just couldn't grasp the concept? That's how it was for me when I was first introduced to the stock market. I wanted to know stocks but it was spoken in a language I just could not comprehend.

When I was younger there were times I had the opportunity to sit with my grandfather while he watched the evening news. I found the news to be interesting and informative with the current events, stories, and gossip. My grandfather enjoyed those segments of the news as he was able to have his opinion and input. However, when it would come to the segment in the news called "Latest in Stock News" I noticed during this segment he didn't pay much attention to it and he had little to no interest. Or maybe he just didn't understand. He just sat and eagerly waited until they made it to the sports segment.

However, the stock segment would intrigue me. I would always watch and listen. I would look at the charts and graphs as they danced across the screen with numbers constantly moving. I could never understand what they were or what they were talking about but it looked exciting. All I knew was that it had to do with money and I knew I liked money.

As I grew older I would look into stocks and investing but it always seemed above my head the more I learned the more it became confusing. Every time I went to learn the stock market I would learn a little and the rest seemed foreign therefore I would give up and try something different.

Being a working American at the time I knew I did not want to work my entire life. I knew working without investing I would not have the retirement I wanted or the lifestyle I wanted to live. With that in mind, I knew I had to figure out a way to invest. I knew the stock market was a great way to do so. All I needed to know was how to invest and how to do it wisely. I became determined to learn the stock market so I could become a wise investor and secure the retirement I dreamed of. In my pursuit to obtain this knowledge, I realized the language of investing was not a simple lingo to understand. I spent countless hours reading and re-reading until it became plain and simple. I then realized that some of the things that seemed so complicated were simple when broken down into common terms. When you learn what these so-called complicated terms mean, you find yourself saying DUH!!! Is that all that means. So in Duh!! It's Just Stocks, I will tell you everything I learned about the stock market, I will explain it to you in a way that you can only say Duh! You will be able to understand and communicate like an investor.

I learned becoming an investor was not as complicated as I made it out to be. You do not need to come from an ivy league school or graduate with a 4.0 at Harvard Business School. This is not rocket science, it's just stock. You simply need to know basic math and have the time to research utilizing some simple easy to use research tools. The key is to know what you're looking for.

Upon completion of this book, I hope that you feel empowered with the basic knowledge of the stock market and terms. You will have the conversational language of the stock market. I hope this information gives you the confidence to consider being a stock market investor and continuing your educational pursuit to invest.

Let's Get Started DUH!!!!

Chapter 1: Why invest?

We all in some way shape or form have financial goals in our life whether it be to send our kids to college, start a business, have disposable income, marriage or purchase a home. We all have some financial goals we want to attain. Saving money or working one job in most circumstances is just not enough to achieve your financial goals. When we operate with the mindset of just working and saving we typically are stretched too thin or we have to give up something. To create additional finances we do not want to give up precious time to do so. Therefore, investing is the best opportunity to achieve financial security through passive income. Stock investing is the best way to achieve passive income without exchanging too much time.

Fidelity investments did a study and found that 88% of millionaires are self-made. The study also discovered that their top assets were investments/capital appreciation, compensation, and employee stock options/profit sharing. Investing in today's economy is the best way to increase your revenue hands down.

Most people do not know how to invest or have big misconceptions about investing. We tend to believe only the rich invest. This is simply not true. Investors are those who are willing to invest their discretionary income into something for a return. An investor is someone willing to take an educated risk for a return. By purchasing and reading this book you have started on your way to investing. As you hope after reading this book you have a better understanding of the basics of stock therefore you expect a return on your investment.

Investing in the stock market is not difficult. It doesn't require a college degree, advanced calculus skills and you don't have to be special just willing.

You can invest in many things such as real estate, businesses, products, ideas, or the stock market. Investing in the stock market is what we will focus on. Investing in the stock market is the easiest investment, it's affordable to start investing, and one of the best passive income streams in the investment arena. The stock market is the number one investment and it is by far the most beneficial place to put your money.

By investing in the stock market you're participating in the overall economy from the business perspective. You will become part of a larger company and allow yourself to benefit from one of America's richest income streams. You will no longer be considered just a consumer, you will become an investor and shareholder of some of the largest companies in the world.

Just like any investment, there are risks in the stock market. However, minimizing risk in the stock market requires obtaining as much knowledge as possible by doing research. Just like in any other investment there are pros and cons. Below please look at the pros and cons of investing below.

PROS	CONS
Grow with the economy- As the economy grows everything else follows. Economic growths create jobs, sales, etc	Risk of losing investment-If a company does bad, investors will sell, sending the stock price down. If you sell, you will lose your initial investment.
Stay ahead of inflation-stocks have an average annualized return of 10%. Better than the average annualized inflation rate	Takes time to research-you must research each company to determine how profitable you think it will be before you buy its stock. You must learn how to read financial statements and annual reports and follow your company's developments in the news.
Easy to buy and sell	Emotional ups and downs- prices rise and fall second-by-second. Individuals tend to buy high, out of greed, and sell low, out of fear.

As you can see in the table there are pros and cons with investing. However, with the right research and time, you can minimize your risk and create a profitable return. The key to risk is management. This simply means knowing what you're investing in and why you're investing in it.

To build wealth for you and your family this can not be achieved by simply saving and working. You may achieve some of the goals you set out but you might have to work extremely hard to obtain them. To give yourself financial freedom consider investing your finances in a place where it can work for you. Financial freedom is attainable with the right knowledge and execution. Don't be afraid!

Stock Facts: Warren Buffet owner of Berkshire Hathaway is the richest stock investor in the world. Warren Buffet began investing in stock at 11 years old.

Key Term: Stock Market is an exchange that allows people to buy and sell stocks of publicly traded companies

Chapter 1 Q & A

I didn't graduate high school. Can I invest?
Yes, you can, it does not require rocket science to invest. You just need basic math skills, patience, a critical eye, and financial tolerance, and time.

Is the stock market a guaranteed profit if I invest?
No. No investment is guaranteed. To minimize your risk and receive a return you must research and invest wisely.

Chapter 2: 400 Year Old Stock Market

Have you ever asked yourself, Self how did they come up with this stock market? Well, the simple answer is when countries began trading with each other there became a need for the stock market. As these countries began to grow and merchants wanted to grow their businesses they realized they did not have the necessary capital as an individual. As a result, these merchants formed partnerships and offered individual shares of the business. This idea was beneficial to struggling businesses looking to grow.

The first stock market goes back to Belgium in the 1400s. Several securities were sold via these stock systems as they called them back in the days including slaves. The current Wall Street in New York City as we know it was created in 1792 from a meeting of 24 stockbrokers under a buttonwood tree.

The stock market is over 400 years old and relied upon by most countries. Businesses use the stock market to raise money by allowing the public to buy shares and corporate bonds in their company. Besides, the stock market regulates other financial assets such as bitcoins, euro, yen, gold, and silver to name just a few.

You might be asking yourself, what does the age of the stock market have to do with investing? Well simple, I want you to understand the credibility of the stock market. This market has been around longer than all of us. This lets you know that the stock market will not go anywhere anytime soon. It is most likely to be here at least another 100 years. So when investing in the market wisely you can have some sort of security knowing the sustainability of the market as a whole when long-term investing.

Over the past 400 plus years, the stock market has made thousands of individuals extremely rich. This was accomplished by simply knowing the right stocks to invest in and how to utilize the stock market for growth, assets, and dividends. This simple passive income seemed like one of America's best kept unhidden secrets sitting in plain sight. The communication barrier between the financial world and the regular individual kept the common person away from this seemingly complicated financial market.

Initially, if you wanted to invest in the stock market you would need to use a stockbroker. A stockbroker is also known as a registered representative or an investment advisor. In previous times stockbrokers were the only individuals who could buy and trade on the stock market. The stockbroker would conduct all the necessary research on a company for a client and then provide recommendations on the trades. Clients did not have access to the resources the stockbrokers possessed which made them valuable.

The use of a stockbroker eliminated a lot of individuals who wanted to participate in the stock market due to the lack of capital. One of the requirements of most investment firms was that the client needed a large amount of capital, the minimum in most cases at that time being $10,000 (this amount varies per brokerage firm). Most individuals did not have this type of cash sparingly or ready to use for investing. Those who had this type of cash did not speak the language of the stockbroker. They either do not participate for lack of understanding or they would have to entrust that the stockbroker would invest their cash properly. Yes, you heard me right, just trust them with your money to do the right thing. RIIIGGHHTT!

Today the stock market has evolved with the times of technology. The everyday individual can now invest in the stock market due to current investment technology and easy access applications like Robinhood, WeBull, TD Ameritrade, and CashApp to name a limited few. These apps are considered self-managed brokerage accounts. The investors' limitation of the need for a stockbroker and large capital is now removed.

With the use of technology, the regular Joe can now participate in a life-changing investment market, So we thought. The limitation remains, how do we speak the language of the investor? How can the regular Joe understand a 400-year-old language that has made so many men wealthy? Simple, by removing the fear and reservation and realizing it's not that complicated. I will break down basic stock terms and lingo that will help you begin to grasp the concept of investing.

You Are Now the Stockbroker

When you begin utilizing a self-managed brokerage account you become your stockbroker. Just like you stockbroker you are responsible for your investments. Though the regular individual now has access to this great investment resource the key now is how to increase your investment and avoid bad investments. This happens with a great deal of research on stocks you are interested in. There are several resources to utilize to research stock. Later on, in the book, we will go over some of these resources and what to look for. To invest in the stock market does not require a college degree or advanced math skills so do not let the research scare you; it's simple to research that will allow you to make smart informed investment decisions. The right research can help you be a wiser, better investor.

Being your own stockbroker also requires you to understand your investment strategies. What your investment goals are and the strategy you plan to utilize to get there. As an investor, you need to know if you are interested in long-term investing, short-term investing, growth, or value. You may be interested in a bit of all. We will go over the basics of all these strategies to give you a conversational understanding and an idea of what may interest you.

Stock Facts: *The first modern stock trade was created in Amsterdam. The Durch East India company was the first* *publicly-traded company to sell stocks and pay dividends to investors.*

Key Terms: *Stockbroker- A broker buys and sells securities on a stock exchange on behalf of a clients*

Chapter 2 Q & A

I only have $100 to invest, is that enough?
Yes, you can invest with as little as $5 there is no minimum to invest. Your investment amount depends on you and the stock you chose.

If I open a self-managed brokerage account am I a financial advisor if I am my own broker?
No. You are allowed to invest for yourself but you can not invest for other people other than your minor family members.

If I open a brokerage account do I need to provide personal information?
Yes, you will need to provide your address date of birth, social security number, bank account information, etc. This is needed as this is a financial transaction that can be taxed.

What strategy should I use?
You will pick your strategy over time. First, you must know why you are investing and your investment goals. Once you know your investment goals you will begin to develop your strategy.

My neighbor knows about stocks can't he just tell me what to buy?

If your neighbor is not a financial advisor I would say No. It's ok to get a recommendation but please do your research and reasoning behind your investment.

Chapter 3: What are stocks?

What are stocks? In the simplest term stock is a company. It represents fractional ownership of a corporation.

Example: If ABC company (corporation) and ABC became a public company and offered fractional ownership of the company now becomes a Stock on the public market.

Stocks are simply companies that have gone public. Public meaning a company that offers shares to be traded freely on the stock exchange to investors for a specific price per share. Public companies are just that public. Once a company goes public, so do its finances, plans, and salaries, and more. Any stock on the market has to publicly report and post all of its financial gains and losses.

 Private companies are not considered stock.

Corporations typically decide to go public to raise money from new investors for new ventures and future growth. Some companies go public to cultivate the company's reputation and brand.

A company can't just wake up one day and say Hey! I want to go public, there is a process. For a company to go public, it has to go through what's called the Initial Public Offering is commonly known as the IPO. New companies coming on to the stock market are called IPOs. This process starts with the company finding a Securities Exchange Commission (SEC) approved investment bank with an underwriter. The underwriter will analyze the company's financials. The company will do what's called a roadshow of pre-market trading. Based on their assessment the offering will be set to go public. Now the company will become a stock.

Just because a company becomes public and now considered stock doesn't mean it will remain on the stock market. WHAT!!!?? I know you were thinking. This can happen in a few different ways. A company can simply choose not to be public anymore and request what's called voluntary delisting. Delisting is a process of removal from the stock market. Another form of delisting is involuntary when a company does not meet the SEC listing requirements. Some of the requirements can be maintaining trading price thresholds, minimum revenue, or shareholder percentage requirements. If you have invested in a company that is being delisted you will receive the amount the stock was worth at the time of delisting based on the number of shares.

Ticker Symbols

Stocks are sold by using what's called a Ticker Symbol (Stock Symbol). Each company is assigned a unique ticker symbol when it goes public. This is how a company is identified on the stock market.

When you buy a share or research a stock you would look up

the company's ticker symbol.

For example Apple (ticker symbol APPL) Tesla (ticker symbol TSLA) Facebook (ticker symbol FB) Netflix (ticker symbol NFLX) Disney ticker symbol DIS)

Putting in the right ticker symbol is important because you want to make sure you purchase and research the right company. There have been instances where the wrong companies have been purchased by utilizing the wrong ticker symbol.

Stock Sectors

When a company goes public it then becomes a stock and is identified under one or more sectors.

Public companies are categorized into what's called "stock sectors". Stock sectors are economic areas where company's share a common or related product or service. Sectors typically share common operating traits such as technology. Companies like Tesla, Uber, Netflix, and Amazon would fall under technology. The reason for this is because they utilize some sort of technology in their business. Within the stock market, there are eleven stock sectors. This represents 11 areas of opportunity to invest. The following are the 11 stock sectors:

1. **Energy**
2. **Basic Materials**
3. **Industrials**
4. **Consumer Discretionary**
5. **Consumer Staples**

6.   **Healthcare**
7.   **Financial**
8.   **Information Technology**
9.   **Communications**
10.   **Utilities**
11.   **Real Estate**

Stock Sectors can play a major part in how you diversify or plan out your investment portfolio. You may not want to put all your stock in ONE BASKET so to speak. You can take a risk if all your stocks are in one sector. Diversification of sectors can minimize the risk of overall loss in your portfolio.

For example: If all of your stocks are in the technology sector and that particular sector is not doing well, there's a possibility that your entire portfolio will take a loss. If you diversify your portfolio with the different sectors, you will have the opportunity to pull in gains from another sector that may have growth while the other sector recovers. Understanding and utilizing the differences in the sectors can minimize your risk and improve your returns.

Stock Myths:

Don't let common stock myths keep you from investing in the stock market. One of the biggest myths is that you will lose all your money if the stock market crashes. That's just not true, what is true is that you will lose your money if you sell off your stocks at a loss. Just because the market crashes does not mean it will not recover. If you maintain your position in your stock when the market recovers you will gain your profits back.

Remember the only way you will lose is if you panic and sell at a loss or if the stock never recovers.

Another stock myth is that the stock market is an exclusive boys club for the rich and wealthy. This is simply not true. To invest in the stock market can take as little as one hundred dollars or less. With today's technology as mentioned in the previous chapter, you have several opportunities and avenues to become an investor. Move over boys club here comes retail!!!

Stock Facts: *The New York Stock Exchange is one of the most conservative markets. No one is allowed to enter the floor without a suit and tie.*

Stock Facts: *Stocks can also become public through what's called a SPAC Special Purpose Acquisition Company. This is done through private investments and it gives a company a chance to skip the IPO process.*

Key Term: *Stock Sectors a group of stocks that are common by industry service and/or products. Stock sectors are used to categorize stocks.*

Chapter 3 Q & A

What if I look up a company and it doesn't have a ticker symbol?

Then most likely the company is not publicly traded. Several popular companies have not gone public.

If I don't know the ticker symbol how do I find it?
You can look up the company by name in your brokerage account or Yahoo finance it will provide you with the ticker symbol.

How can I find companies I may want to invest in?
You can start with the things you use. Your utility company, your cellphone company, etc and see if they offer stocks. Stocks are all around you, don't be afraid just to look up a company. Once you start there you will see other companies you may want to research.

Chapter 4: Stock Shares

Now that you understand that a stock is just simply an investable public company, now you need to understand how you can own a part of that company/stock. Ownership of stock requires simply purchasing your shares.

To buy and sell a stock you need a brokerage account. A brokerage account holds your financial assets (i.e. your funds for trading) it is a security account on behalf of the investor. There are a couple of types of brokerage accounts. One is like we discussed in the earlier chapter, a brokerage company that will hold your funds and buys and trades on your behalf and they charge a fee to do so. Remember the stockbroker. The other is the self-managed brokerage account where you can research, buy and sell stocks for yourself. We will focus on self-managed brokerage accounts. First, let's understand how stocks are bought and sold.

Shares

What are shares? you may be asking. Well, that's easy, it's just a small piece of the pie to put it plain and simple. Shares give you small ownership of a major company.

Stocks are divided up into equal parts called shares. Shares are equity ownership interest in a stock. Owning a share of stock gives you a certificate of ownership therefore you become a shareholder.

To become a shareholder of stock all you need is to own one share of a particular stock. Shareholders are simply someone who owns one or more shares of a stock or equity. There are a few benefits of being a stockholder one of course is return on your investment. Depending on the stock as a shareholder you can receive discounts on certain items and/or perks on services. This will all depend on the company and what they offer their shareholders. As a shareholder, you are technically part of the business and one of the benefits of this is shareholders get to vote on certain company issues and policy. Also, you receive annual reports and have the option to attend shareholder meetings where the company will go over its financials and future goals and projections. And of course, if the company grows you grow either through a share price increase or dividend payout. You must admit being a shareholder and part-owner of a major company is pretty cool.

Price Per Share

As mentioned previously each stock offers shares of their company to interested shareholders. However, to become a shareholder you must first purchase the shares. Share prices can range from .59 cents to $30,000 and up. Each company has a different amount per share based on the value of the company. To purchase a share of stock, you must pay the cost of the share price. See the example below:

> **Example:** *If ABC Stock is priced at $5 per share and I want to buy 10 shares of ABC stock I would pay $50 for 10 shares of ABC stock.*
>
> *If ABC stock is $5 per share and I want to own 1 share I would simply pay $5.*
>
> *You will always take the share price and multiply it by the number of shares you would like to purchase.*

The price per share is used to determine the company/stock market capitalization simply put how much the company is worth. Companies with higher value (worth more money) will most likely have higher share prices. This is not always true for all companies. Some companies have a lower price but a high value simply because they may pay out a higher dividend that keeps the share price lower.

Fractional Shares

You can also purchase what's called fractional shares. Fractional shares are a small percentage of a single share. If you are unsure about the stock market this is an affordable way for you to participate at your own pace.

You would purchase fractional shares in dollar amounts and not share prices. Meaning if you want to own ABC company and the share price is currently $50 you can own a tenth of the share by purchasing it for $5. You will not own a full share but a partial share (i.e. fractional). The benefits of fractional shares allow you to participate in stock for a minimal amount.

If you want to start investing and getting yourself into an investment position you may consider fractional shares.

Market Capitalization (Market Cap)

Market cap can be used to help investors research a company. Market cap can tell you the size of a company as well as the value. The market cap can help you with comparisons when looking at multiple companies in the same sector.

Understanding the market capitalization of a stock is one way to help you determine if you want to own the company. However, just because a company has a lower market cap does not mean it is not a great company. The market cap simply determines what a company is worth on the open market (stock market). The way the market cap is determined is by taking the company's outstanding shares and multiplying them by the share price. See the example below.

> **Example:** *ABC stock has 50,000 outstanding shares (shares not sold) the current share price for ABC stock is $5. The current market cap for ABC stock would be $250,000   (5 x 50,000= 250,000) pretty simple stuff*

Just like stock sectors, companies are also identified by their market cap. You have a large-cap, mid-cap, small-cap, and micro-cap company. Based on the value of a company they will fall under a particular market cap. Large-cap companies tend to range in value of $10 - 20 billion dollars. Companies like Amazon, Tesla, Facebook, and Apple would be large-cap companies. You will find most of your larger-cap companies in the Standard & Poor's (S&P 500) Index.

When doing your research you will hear a lot about market cap, just make a note this is the value of the company on the public market.

Key Term: Market Capitalization is the market value of a publicly-traded company Market cap is equal to the share price multiplied by the outstanding shares.

Chapter 4 Q & A

Is it a minimum number of shares I need to buy to become a shareholder?

You need to buy 1 share of the company to make you a shareholder. In some cases you can have a fractional share this also makes you a shareholder

I have a stock I like and I want to buy it but I only have

enough for one share should I wait?

No. If you like the stock and it's at a price you like then I would buy it even if it is one share. I would get a position in the stock. You can begin to build a portfolio with one share

Is it possible to find stock with share prices under $5?

Yes, stocks under $5 are considered a penny stock. There are cases where these stocks are good and capable of growing. Keep in mind on 9/20/2010 Tesla shares were trading at $4.13 it now trades above $600 per share. Amazon at one point was also trading around $6 per share now it is over $3000 per share.

Chapter 5: Value, Growth & Dividend Stocks

When buying stock and deciding on your strategy you will need to look at growth stock, value stock, and dividend stock. Though all three may have similarities the strategy of the stock is different. Value focuses more on longevity and sustainability, growth is focused on growing the company and stock, and dividends focus on sharing the profit with the shareholder.

When deciding on buying stocks one of the things you need to ask yourself is, do I want growth stocks, dividend stocks, value stock, or a mix of all three? We will briefly go over the difference between the two and the pros and cons of both.

Dividends

What are dividends?

Dividends are payments to shareholders of publicly traded companies. The amount of a dividend may vary but this is determined by the board of directors and the company's actual earnings. When a company has profits they take a portion of those profits and distribute them to shareholders which are called dividends.

All companies do not pay out dividends to their shareholders. Some companies are designed to be growth stocks, therefore, they reinvest all profits back into the company which increases the share price over time, Companies that pay out dividends typically do not grow as fast per share however they pay out dividends to their shareholders as profit increases.

Dividends are usually paid out quarterly to the shareholders. The board of directors approves the amount of the dividend and when it will be paid to the shareholders. Dividends are paid out to shareholders based on the number of shares they own. See the example below.

> **Example:** *ABC stock will pay a .75 cents dividend. You own 5 shares of ABC Stock your dividend payout will be $3.75 (5 shares x .75 dividend payout = $3.75 total dividend payment to the shareholder)*

The most common dividend is the cash dividend shown in the example and the most popular. However, there are a few different types of dividends a company can pay. Companies can offer shareholders stock dividends. Instead of paying out cash companies can offer additional stocks as dividends. Stock dividends should not be confused with DRIP (dividend reinvestment programs); this is where the cash dividend is reinvested into the stock sometimes at a discount. Special dividends are not regularly paid dividends but often a one-time payment is given to shareholders after immense profit over time.

To receive your dividend payment, you must own the shares of stock before the ex-dividend date. The ex-dividend date is the day the stock is trading without dividend value. To receive your dividend payment, you must own the stock before the ex-dividend date or you will not receive a dividend until the next quarter.

Growth Stocks

Growth stocks are companies that have a high potential to outperform the market's average growth. These companies usually anticipate a high growth in revenue stream at a fast pace which will increase the share price. Growth stocks typ[ically reinvest their profits into the company for future innovations or investments to help the company grow at a rapid speed. Growth stocks are usually innovative and lead the pack in their industries to have some sort of unique service, product, or delivery of service or product. Because growth stocks tend to outperform the market they either pay an extremely low dividend to none at all. Growth stocks offer their investors growth through capital gains.

Growth stocks typically provide a higher capital return and are typically for the investor who wants to see a quicker return. However, these stocks are also extremely volatile and risky meaning they can fall as fast as they rise. Having growth stock in your portfolio is risky however the profit margins if you purchase at the right time can be tremendous.

I typically use my growth stock for a large profit margin. I keep them for at least a year. But my strategy is to use those returns to buy additional stocks. For example, I purchased Novavax at $42 per share and it ran to $298 per share. I sold 1 share to receive a return and bought 10 shares of another but it provided me the opportunity to buy into another stock at a great position from my profits.

Dividend Stocks

Dividend stocks are typically older more mature companies with a history of distributing earnings. These companies are well established in their sectors and typically pay their shareholders a portion of their profits. Dividend stocks can provide a stable passive income stream to shareholders

Dividend stocks are less volatile and typically for the investor who has low-risk tolerance. Dividend stocks can also offer capital gains along with dividends. Dividend-paying stocks are usually established businesses that can predict their cash flows and can also increase the share they return to investors from their profit.

Having dividend stock in your portfolio is extremely smart. You have some investors who will not buy a stock that doesn't pay a dividend. Dividend stocks are considered the stock that pays you. There are several ways to survive off your dividend alone if you have the right capital. For example, I use PFE (Pfizer) as my dividend play. PFE is currently $36.68, I bought in at

$30.17. As you can see the growth is not extreme. I bought 300 shares of PFE which cost at the time $9051. Their dividend payments average around $0.85 per share paid out quarterly four times a year. So every 3 months I receive a deposit of around $255 because I own 300 shares. This is $1020 deposited into my brokerage account. This is an 11.2% return on my investment in a year. This is more than banks. I can use it for savings, reinvesting, or vacationing.

Now let's talk about share price. I bought my shares at $30.17 it is currently $36.68 so I also received a growth in share price if I chose to sell my return would be $1953. This is just an example of how dividend stocks can pay you back.

When considering what type of investor you want to be you will need to consider growth stock, dividend stocks, or both. As you see there are benefits in both. There is no right or wrong in this choice; you simply need to know what your financial goals are and determine how you want to get there.

Value Stocks

Value stocks are companies that usually have longevity and sustainability. One of the other attractive traits of value stocks are they are typically underpriced in comparison to the fundamentals. Value stocks sometimes may get confused with growth stocks but they are different. A value stock is just like it sounds. Imagine you were in love with a shoe that you know is worth $100 but you find them for $60 that is considered valuable as the shoe is worth $100

Stock Facts: The Dutch East India Company (VOA) was the first to pay dividends to shareholders in 1602. They paid dividends for 200 years.

Chapter 5 Q & A

If a company doesn't pay a dividend is it a bad company?
No. Dividends are not guaranteed by all companies. Some companies choose to reinvest profits into the company for growth. Growth stocks typically do not pay dividends however some do.

Can a company cancel a dividend?
Yes, a company can cancel dividends this can be temporary or forever. Temporary is usually considered as a suspended dividend. Canceling a dividend would be forever. This usually happens if there is a major problem in the stock and they need to keep the profit for sustainability.

If a company misses a dividend payment will I receive two payments next time?
No, A missed dividend payment is a loss of a dividend payment. Your next dividend payment will reflect a percentage of the shareholder profit only.

How do I receive my dividend payment?

Dividend payments are paid out quarterly or annual and payouts are deposited into your brokerage account.

Chapter 6: Understanding ETFs & Bonds

There are different ways of investing and different investment strategies. Sometimes you are not sure what stock to invest in or what strategy you would like to use. Nevertheless, you know that you want to invest. This is where Exchange Traded Funds (ETF's) and Bonds can be of use to the new investor.

Exchange-Traded Funds(ETF's)

Exchange-Traded Funds were introduced onto the market in the1990s. ETFs were intended to provide investors an opportunity at passive income through index funds. Index funds and ETFs follow a certain preset rule to track a specified group of underlying investments.

ETFs are a group of stocks under one ticker symbol. ETFs can trade assets, commodities, sectors, or an index.

In the previous chapter, we discussed finding stocks in different sectors. Sectors are economic categories that host similar products or services. If you are not sure which company you would like to invest in you can invest in an ETF. Some ETFs are structured to host multiple companies in similar sectors under one ticker symbol. For example, if you were interested in the airline industry and did not know which company to invest in you could simply buy shares in the JETS ETF. The

JETS ETF is an exchange-traded fund that provides investors access to the airline industry. JETS has multiple airline stocks within the one ETF such as American Airlines, Southwest, United, and a host of others. If you were indecisive on which airline to choose you can purchase the JETS ETF and own a small portion of multiple airlines. There are several ETFs that you can choose from that focus on different sectors. If you can not make a decision on a particular stock, but know the sector that you may be interested in, look for the ETF that hosts the stocks you may want to own in that sector. Below see an example of JETS ETF holdings.

Not only are ETFs great for owning a group of stocks all at once, but it's also an affordable way to own expensive stocks you may not be able to afford. For example, if you were interested in owning Amazon (AMZ) it would cost you $3028 per share as of today. If you are not able to afford Amazon outright you may consider purchasing an ETF that has holdings in Amazon. An ETF such as XLY Consumer Discretionary that will cost $166 per share as of today, will allow you to have an investment in Amazon at a more affordable price.

Similar to regular stock an ETF can payout dividends and some ETFs have growth stocks. One of the great things about an ETF is that it will pick stocks based on the fundamentals or

Name	Symbol	% Assets
Southwest Airlines Co	LUV	10.92%
American Airlines Group Inc	AAL	10.54%
Delta Air Lines Inc	DAL	10.05%
United Airlines Holdings Inc	UAL	9.56%
Allegiant Travel Co	ALGT	4.99%
Spirit Airlines Inc	SAVE	4.85%
Alaska Air Group Inc	ALK	4.53%
JetBlue Airways Corp	JBLU	4.25%
SkyWest Inc	SKYW	3.42%
Air Canada Class B	AC.TO	3.31%

a particular investment strategy. This makes it easy on the investor who may not have the time to do the research or develop a strategy. On the other hand, an ETF will charge a small fee to manage the fund. This fee is very minimal and can go unnoticed. The fee is to maintain a profitable portfolio and this requires conducting extensive research you may not have the time to do.

Bonds

Bonds are considered a safe investment because they come with less risk than individual stocks. However, bonds are not stocks. With stocks, you own a small portion of the company.

Bonds are loans given to a company or government agency by the investor (you). You become a creditor when you purchase a bond. Companies will offer up bonds to raise money for the company operations, projects or simply to get out of debt.

Companies offer bonds to raise capital for many reasons, fund a project or company operations. Though a company can go directly to a bank for this capital they choose to offer bonds. Bonds are more attractive as they have fewer restrictions on companies and offer better rates than direct bank loans. Issuing a bond on the open market for a company is less comparative.

When you purchase a bond as stated you become a creditor and/or debt holder. I know you may be wondering, how do I make money off debt? Simple, when you purchase the bond the company will agree to pay face value plus interest over the term of the bond. Bonds are purchased with a maturity date similar to any loan. This date is the time you will hold the bond. Over this period, the company will make interest payments to you bi-annually or annually depending on the bond agreement. When the bond matures the company will pay you the face value of the bond. The profit that you will receive will be the interest payments made throughout the bond plus face value.

When considering bonds an investor should look at a few key details about the bond. The first one is interest rates. You would like to know what interest will be paid to you for the purchase of the bond. The interest paid out can vary; it all depends on the bond and prevailing interest rates at the time. Also, when purchasing a bond you should find out if the interest rate is fixed or floating. A fixed-rate bond is exactly as it sounds fixed. Fixed rates do not change over the term of the bond. There are pros and cons to fixed-rate bonds. One of the pros is if the market interest rates drop you will be locked in with your bond rate. However, if the market rates rise you will not benefit from the interest rate increase. If they offer fixed rates this is guaranteed payments. Floating rates can fluctuate up or down. With floating rates, you can take advantage of the market rates as they increase however you will also be subject to decrease if the market rates go down.

The maturity date is also another key factor when choosing a bond. The maturity date is the day the bond becomes due and payable to the investor. The maturity date can be short, medium, or long term. Short-term bonds are typically within 1-4 years. The short-term bond is the most sought after. Short-term bonds offer less risk and closer to capital return. Medium-term bonds can be from 2 - 10 years. Long-term bonds are typically 10 years or more.

Bonds can also be Callable or Redeemable. These are bonds that can be purchased by the borrower before the maturity date. You want to find out if the bond you are purchasing has a call provision. This gives the borrower the option to buy back the bond before the maturity date to refinance at a cheaper rate or cancel the debt. Bonds that have a call provision typically pay higher interest rates. They also usually have a higher face value. However, if the bond is called, investors typically end up with lower interest rate bonds.

In addition to maturity dates and interest rates you also want to know why the company is offering a bond. It's important to find out the stability of the company. You want to know if they are on the verge of bankruptcy as this can put your bond at risk. Though with a bond you are a creditor and your bond is considered senior debt which is usually paid out first.

Bond Facts: The first bond sold was in 2400BC in Nippur, Mesopotamia. The principal guarantee was grain.

Key Term: Maturity date is the day the payment of the bond becomes due and payable by the borrower.

Remember

1. The interest paid on the bond
2. The maturity date
3. The cost of the bond
4. Stability of the company
5. Why did the company offer the bond

Chapter 6 Q & A

If I have an ETF will I receive a dividend payment?
Yes, you will receive a portion of the dividend payment.

Can I buy multiple shares of the same ETF?

Yes, ETFs are traded like a stock. You can buy as many shares as you like.

If I own bonds and ETFs will that be considered a diversified portfolio?

Yes, being that you have bonds and ETF you have diversified your funds in two different markets.

Can I sell my bond before the maturity date?

Yes, you can but you may have to pay a fee to do so.

Chapter 7: Confusing Data: Understanding The Summary

I know one of the things that are extremely frustrating about stocks is not knowing what everything means that you are looking at. In this chapter, I will go over a few of the common things you will see when you first look up a ticker symbol and what they mean.

Understanding the data is important to your research. However, you do not need to understand everything. Certain pieces of data and information are for particular strategies or investment styles. Day traders and options traders review the data differently than regular stock investors. So don't let the information intimidate you. The key is to know what type of investor you are and focus on that data. You will learn more as you go along.

Below you will see information from a stock I pulled up on Yahoo Finance, a very popular place to research and review stocks. As you can see just on the initial summary page there is a lot of information. I'm sure to some it may look complicated and confusing, however, it's not that confusing or hard to understand once broken down.

Previous Close	12.15	Market Cap	49.395B
Open	12.16	Beta (5Y Monthly)	1.21
Bid	12.40 x 34100	PE Ratio (TTM)	N/A
Ask	12.41 x 36100	EPS (TTM)	-0.32
Day's Range	12.11 - 12.43	Earnings Date	Apr 26, 2021 - Apr 30, 2021
52 Week Range	4.17 - 13.62	Forward Dividend & Yield	N/A (N/A)
Volume	25,891,247	Ex-Dividend Date	Jan 29, 2020
Avg. Volume	82,392,783	1y Target Est	11.93

1D 5D 1M 6M YTD 1Y 5Y Max   Full screen

12.50
12.41
12.35

12.20
12.15

12.05

10 AM   12 PM   02 PM

Trade prices are not sourced from all markets

The first thing you will notice is the share price or price per share, which for this particular stock it is **$12.41**. This is the cost the stock is currently trading at. The **+0.26** is the amount the stock has increased so far that trading day which is a **+2.17%** increase. As you watch the stock market you will notice these numbers change throughout the trading day.

Now let us review the other information on this summary page.

The previous close is what the stock closed at on the previous trading day. You will see for this particular stock closed at $12.15 per share.

Open is what the share price began trading when the market opened on the current trading day $12.16.

<u>**A bid**</u> is a price the investor is willing to pay for a particular stock.

The <u>**Ask**</u> is what the market/brokers are willing to sell the stock for.

<u>**Day's Range**</u> is the price of the stock that has fluctuated throughout the current trading day. This is usually good for those wanting to see how the stock moves throughout a trading day.

The <u>**52-week range**</u> is the price of the stock has fluctuated throughout the trading year. This is where you will see the highest price per share and the lowest price per share the stock has traded within the current year. You may sometimes see this listed as 52 weeks high and 52 week low.

<u>**Volume**</u> is the number of trades happening on the stock on that particular day. High volumes indicate a lot of activity and movement in the stock. Low volume means there is not much interest. I like stock with 100,000 plus in volume is good activity.

<u>**Average Volume**</u> is the trading volume activity over a period of time.

<u>**Market Cap (market capitalization)**</u> is the current valuation of the company. This company is currently valued at 49.395 billion dollars. This is calculated by the number of outstanding shares and the current share price. Companies can be large,

mid, or small-cap companies. The market cap can help with your research understanding the value of the company in comparison to others in the sector.

Beta is also commonly known as the volatility of a stock. **Beta** tells you how the stock is moving within the current market. Anything over 1.0 is considered volatile. This company **Beta** is currently at 1.21 meaning there has been some significant price movement. This can be up or down movement.

P/E Ratio is the price to earnings ratio of a stock. This is used in valuing a company in regards to if they are overvalued or undervalued. A company with a high **P/E ratio** could be an indicator that the company is overvalued. When the **P/E ratio** is N/A this could be that there is no data which typically happens for new companies such as IPOs. The other reason the **P/E ratio** will be at N/A status is that the company earnings are negative therefore returns a N/A.

EPS is the stock's earnings per share. **EPS** is the company's profit divided by outstanding shares. **EPS** is the company's profit per share.

Earnings Date is the date the company will release its next earnings report.

Forward Dividend & Yield is the estimated dividend for the coming year.

Ex-Dividend Date is the date the stock starts trading with the dividend value. Meaning if you purchase the stock after the **ex-dividend date** you will not be entitled to a dividend payout. If you purchased before the date you would receive the dividend.

1 yr. target estimate is the price point that is estimated from the year to the current date.

The things you see in this Yahoo Finance summary you will see in many different tools you use to look up stock. These are the more common pieces of data used to begin your research. There are several reports and several tools this should get you started so that you can ease into your stock research journey.

What to look for in your research

When you start using the data for research and begin to look up a company there are a few things I would like you to look for. One of them being the overall company product and mission. You want to look at the overview of the company when they were established, do they have a solid product or service, what are the product goals.

The next thing you want to look at is who manages the company. Who is the CEO? This is important as this is the person that will drive the company to its goals. You want to make sure he has the experience and track record to do so. You also want to look at the other management heads to see who their support is. Where the CEO lacks they may fill the void.

You also want to look at the company's financials. You want to know if they have a strong balance sheet. This being debt to income ratio. How much debt does the company have? Does the company have a great cash flow and can they sustain in the event of an emergency or crash? Also, look at the earning data to see if they were consistent with meeting their earnings expectations. This is important for our dividend investors.

You also want to know where they stand in their sector. Find out who are the competing companies and what they look like compared to your interested company. It's always important to know who the leader is in a sector. You may not be able to afford that stock but you want to get as close to the leader as possible.

Lastly, I would look up the current news on the stock and the sector. It is important to know what is going on within a sector just as much as the individual stock. Looking up the current news will help you do this. This will give you information on the sector itself and will report if there are challenges, demand, or failure. All this may affect your stock and its growth.

These are just a few things to look for to get you started on your research journey. This is key information to your investment you would want to know. Only invest in a company if you can say the name of the CEO, know the financial health of the company, and know who the leader is in the sector know thou competition. Always keep up with the news.

Price Point & Personal Value

Once you conduct your research you should either love the company and be ready to invest or move on or put it on your watchlist. If you are looking to invest you would want to put a personal value on the company. This means what you feel the price per share should be based on your personal value. For example, a company may be currently trading at $150, but after research, you feel the price per share should be $125. This is your personal value.

Now that you have your personal value established you want to identify your price point or buy-in price. This is the price you are willing to pay for the stock per share. Though you value the company at $125 per share your buy-in price may be $115 - $130 per share. This means you are comfortable purchasing shares at this price. Now a company may have a share price at $150 per share and after research, you may discover that is a good price point and purchase your shares at that time and that's ok too.

It is very critical to have your value and buy-in price for a company. You want to feel comfortable with your investment and return.

Watchlist

After developing your buy-in price and price point you want to be able to keep track of these stocks. In your brokerage account, you can create what is called a watchlist. This is a list of stocks that you would like to follow for one reason or another. The main reason you will create a watchlist is so that when and if a stock hits your price point you want to know so that you can purchase at that time. As we discussed stocks move rapidly your stock may only hit your price point for that day or even that hour and then the opportunity is lost. Until the next time if any.

You also want to create a watchlist of stocks that you intend to research so that you can see the movement and receive notifications on how the stocks are doing. For me, this serves as a little reminder to do my research.

Tools For Research

As mentioned Yahoo Finance is a great tool to utilize for looking up a company. But there are other tools and resources you can utilize to look up a company.

One of the first places you can go for your research would be the company's website. Every public company has an investor tab on its website. If you go to this tab you will find the companies publicly reported information. You will find their SEC filing their financials and other reporting materials.

Market Watch is another tool I like to use for research. There are a lot of information, analysis, and financials. Market Watch also keeps up with all the current news information on the overall stock market.

Watching the news is also important. CNBC is my favorite source of stock news. Finding a business channel to watch and put your knowledge into practice will help you get an understanding of the market and how it works as a whole. Also, we want to keep up with sector news and updates.

You can also do some research on the platform you use for trading. Webull, RobinHood, and CashApp have some information on stocks but can be limited on the information it provides therefore using other sources can be helpful. TD Ameritrade and Etrade also have great reporting tools and data you can use for trading. But keep in mind these platforms are a bit more complicated to use for a beginner in my opinion.

Key Terms: Personal Price Point is the amount you are willing to pay per share of a stock

Chapter 7 Q & A

How long should I research a stock before I buy it?

That's totally up to you. Once you conduct your research you will come up with a comfortable price point you want to purchase the stock for.

Where can I find information on the company financials?

You can find the financials on Yahoo finance. You can also find the company financials on their website under the investor tab.

Where can I find who the CEO is and their background?

You can find this on their website in the about section or executive team. You can also Google the company and find the CEO. You should review their bio, news articles, and previous accomplishments

What should I look for in my research?

You want to look at the product or services to see if it is sustainable. You want to look at the CEO and management team. You want to see their track record to ensure they can manage the company to success and you want to make sure they have the funds to sustain so you want to look over their financials.

Chapter 8: Stocks and Taxes

When you invest in the stock market you're investing for one real reason, a profit. We are all looking for a return on our investment. However, when we reap the benefits we have to pay the piper.

When you make a profit in the stock market that is considered income in the eyes of the Internal Revenue Service (IRS). Therefore, just like with any income you are required to pay taxes on that income. The IRS will charge you a tax called capital gains. This is based on just like it sounds your capital gains. But there are several different factors on how this is charged and we will go over those factors in this chapter.

On the other side if you have losses you may have a tax write off which is considered a capital loss. In some cases, you may have losses in the stock market and these losses may offset some of your capital gains. So you must keep this in mind when you are selling your stock for profit or losses.

Now, let's understand what is considered a profit. If you have stocks and they have increased by $1000 and you have not sold those stocks this is not considered profit. You are only subject to tax after you sell the stock and take the profit. This is considered realized capital gains, meaning you have actually acquired your profit. You only pay taxes on stocks you have sold at a profit. You do not pay taxes on stocks in your portfolio. Same with a loss, when you sell the stock at a loss then it will become a tax write-off, a realized capital loss.

The capital gains tax will be determined based on how long you held your stock before profit. You may have a long-term tax or a short-term tax. If you hold a stock for more than 1 year (1 year in a day) this would be considered a long-term tax. Long-term tax can be between 0%-15% tax on profit which is preferred. Short-term tax is any stock sold at a profit in under 1 year. Short-term tax will fall under income and can be taxed up to 37% on profitable gains. It is wise to try to hold your stocks for more than 1 year to avoid a higher tax. If you sell your stocks before the year is up, keep in mind you will be taxed based on your current tax bracket based on your income.

If you have chosen stocks that pay out dividends you will have to report this income on your tax return. If you have a qualified dividend company you will be charged the long-term capital gains tax. Non-qualified dividend companies will be taxed based on your income tax bracket.

Though investing in the stock market is a great way to create a secure passive income, you must understand just like with all income in our country a tax will be charged. The amount of tax is all up to you depending on how you invest. When investing consider long term or short term. Also, look at the profit you are taking and is it with the tax that may be associated with it.

Key Terms: *Capital Gains are the tax the IRS will assess on all stock profit. Profit is only assessed based on the sale of a stock "realized capital gains"*

Chapter 8 Q & A

I did not sell my stock. Do I have to pay taxes on it?

No. You only pay taxes on stocks you sell. If you have not sold your stock you do not have realized profits.

Will I receive tax paperwork?

Yes. Your brokerage company will have your tax forms for you. They will email or mail it to you or you can simply pull them up in your account.

Chapter 9: The Emotions of An Investor

Now let's be honest we all at some point are emotionally attached to our finances. No individual wants to worry about their finances. Financial stress is one of America's biggest stressors. So to become an investor with high emotional tolerance, you must understand the potential emotional ups and downs and how to cope with them.

First things first, you never invest with money that you need. You should only use investable funds. Meaning do not use your bill money in hopes of hitting it big before the bills are due. It simply doesn't work like that. You must allocate funds to use for investing. My recommendation is to use funds that you can part with for at least 18 months. I guarantee you if you use money that you need you're going to be high in emotions and you will not make wise decisions, especially if you are highly emotional and in need.

Emotions can run high when investing especially if you are actively watching the market. The stock market is constantly moving. Stocks can go up and down within hours. The key to managing your emotions is knowing the market. Having an understanding of the market and that there are highs and lows.

You must understand that stocks can go up or down for several reasons. You need to be able to determine if the stock is moving down due to overall market movement or if the stock going down due to the individual company itself.

Stocks can go down due to nationwide issues that can affect the economy overall, such as interest rates, COVID-19, riots, wars, change in leadership, etc. any one of these things can have an effect on the stock market as a whole. These issues can cause a decrease or increase in the market.

As an investor, you need to have an understanding of how nationwide issues can affect the market and move accordingly. For example, COVID-19 caused a nationwide quarantine. This resulted in the entire market dropping. When this happened I had to become strategic. I bought stocks while they were low and affordable. Stocks I knew I would not be able to afford otherwise. My strategy was to buy what I called "stay at home" stocks as my growth and then I bought stocks that would recover after the quarantine for a long-term hold. I bought Netflix, FedEx, DocuSign, and Peloton as my stay-at-home stocks. I knew people would need to depend on delivery and entertainment of some sort. I also bought some airline stock, banks, and Disney for my long-term opening stocks, as I felt when the quarantine was lifted people would travel and look for entertainment. With this diversity during the quarantine, I made a 456% return on my investments. I was able to do this solely by understanding the market highs and lows. I did not panic and sell off my current stocks. I looked for an opportunity.

This is why it is important to maintain your emotions when stocks are moving as stated they can move for several reasons. Another reason could be something within the company. For example, a car company can have a recall on a mechanical part this may cause the stock to drop temporarily. This is not a reason to panic or sell. You must keep your emotions in check and truly understand why you're investing. As mentioned in the previous chapter you must believe in what you're investing in to have a high emotional tolerance.

Another big emotion in the stock market is called FOMO (fear of missing out). This is when an investor sees a particular stock rising and they are afraid it will rise too fast they buy instantly without research. Or the stock has lots of hype behind it and they purchase simply because of the hype. Please don't get caught in the FOMO. Please keep in mind stocks move up and they move down, you will always have an opportunity to buy in, you just have to be strategic. You have to understand the day traders. If the day traders are in stock it can cause the stock to rise quickly which is inflating the stock. However, if it's a day trader stock once the traders sell off the stock it will immediately drop. FOMO can cause you to buy an inflated stock and ultimately lose a lot of money.

The more knowledge you obtain about how the market works, you will become less emotional concerning your investments. You will be able to invest noting your managed risk. You will be an investor with a clear understanding of the company's finances, product, and sustainability. Therefore you will not invest with your emotions but with your gained knowledge. This is what separates successful long-term investors from the "gamified retail investor."

Key Terms: FOMO fear of missing out.

Chapter 9 Q & A

Should I save to purchase stock?

Yes, I would allocate a specific pot of money dedicated to stocks. This way you are not using the money you need for your daily living.

How can I control my FOMO?

Simply by doing your research. It's easy to get excited in the stock market. Just keep in mind your goal is profit and FOMO can cause you not to have a profit on your investment.

My stock has dropped, but I know it's a great company. What should I do?

If you know the company is great and you believe the drop is temporary I would buy more stock if you can and keep the stocks you have.

Common Stock Terms

1. **BUY-** To purchase or secure the stock

2. **SELL-** Getting rid of the shares you purchased

3. **BID-** What you are willing to pay for a Stock

4. **ASK-** What the seller is looking to receive for their Stock

5. **DIVIDEND-** Portion of a company's earnings that are paid to shareholders

6. **DRIP-** Dividend reinvestment program

7. **BULL MARKET-** This is the belief the Stock market prices will rise

8. **BEAR MARKET-** IS the belief that the Stock market prices will decline

9. **VOLATILITY-** This is how fast the stock will move up or down

10. **IPO-** Initial Public Offering a NEW company coming to the Stock Market

11. **VOLUME-** Number of Shares being traded daily

12. **EPS-** Earnings Per Share

13. **SECTOR-** Category that stocks are divided into based on their common service or product

Chapter Q & A

Chapter 1 Q & A

I didn't graduate high school. Can I invest?
Yes, you can, it does not require rocket science to invest. You just need basic math skills, patience, a critical eye, and financial tolerance, and time.

Is the stock market a guaranteed profit if I invest?
No. No investment is guaranteed. To minimize your risk and receive a return, you must research and invest wisely.

Chapter 2 Q & A

I only have $100 to invest, is that enough?
Yes, you can invest with as little as $5 there is no minimum to invest. Your investment amount depends on you and the stock you chose.

If I open a self-managed brokerage account am I a financial advisor if I am my own broker?
No. You are allowed to invest for yourself but you can not invest for other people other than your minor family members.

If I open a brokerage account do I need to provide personal information?
Yes, you will need to provide your address date of birth, social security number, bank account information, etc. This is needed as this is a financial transaction that can be taxed.

What strategy should I use?

You will pick your strategy over time. First, you must know why you are investing and your investment goals. Once you know your investment goals you will begin to develop your strategy.

My neighbor knows about stocks can't he just tell me what to buy?

If your neighbor is not a financial advisor I would say No. It's ok to get recommendations but please do your research and reasoning behind your investment.

<u>**Chapter 3 Q & A**</u>

What if I look up a company and it doesn't have a ticker symbol?

Then most likely the company is not publicly traded. Several popular companies have not gone public.

If I don't know the ticker symbol how do I find it?

You can look up the company by name in your brokerage account or Yahoo finance it will provide you with the ticker symbol.

How can I find companies I may want to invest in?

You can start with the things you use. Your utility company, your cellphone company, etc and see if they offer stocks. Stocks are all around you, don't be afraid just to look up a company. Once you start there you will see other companies you may want to research.

<u>**Chapter 4 Q & A**</u>

Is it a minimum number of shares I need to buy to become a shareholder?

You need to buy 1 share of the company to make you a shareholder. In some cases you can have a fractional share this also makes you a shareholder

I have a stock I like and I want to buy it but I only have enough for one share should I wait?

No. If you like the stock and it's at a price you like then I would buy it even if it is one share. I would get a position in the stock. You can begin to build a portfolio with one share

Is it possible to find stock with share prices under $5?

Yes, stocks under $5 are considered a penny stock. There are cases where these stocks are good and capable of growing. Keep in mind on 9/20/2010 Tesla shares were trading at $4.13 it now trades above $600 per share. Amazon at one point was also trading around $6 per share now it is over $3000 per share.

If a company doesn't pay a dividend is it a bad company?

No. Dividends are not guaranteed by all companies. Some companies choose to reinvest profits into the company for growth. Growth stocks typically do not pay dividends however some do.

Can a company cancel a dividend?

Yes, a company can cancel dividends this can be temporary or forever. Temporary is usually considered as a suspended dividend. Canceling a dividend would be forever. This usually happens if there is a major problem in the stock and they need to keep the profit for sustainability.

If a company misses a dividend payment will I receive two payments next time?

No, A missed dividend payment is a loss of a dividend payment. Your next dividend payment will reflect a percentage of the shareholder profit only.

How do I receive my dividend payment?

Dividend payments are paid out quarterly or annual and payouts are deposited into your brokerage account.

Chapter 6 Q & A

If I have an ETF will I receive a dividend payment?

Yes, you will receive a portion of the dividend payment.

Can I buy multiple shares of the same ETF?

Yes, ETFs are traded like a stock. You can buy as many shares as you like.

If I own bonds and ETFs will that be considered a diversified portfolio?

Yes, being that you have bonds and ETF you have diversified your funds in two different markets.

Can I sell my bond before the maturity date?

Yes, you can but you may have to pay a fee to do so.

<u>**Chapter 7 Q & A**</u>

How long should I research a stock before I buy it?

That's totally up to you. Once you conduct your research you will come up with a comfortable price point you want to purchase the stock for.

Where can I find information on the company financials?

You can find the financials on Yahoo finance. You can also find the company financials on their website under the investor tab.

Where can I find who the CEO is and their background?

You can find this on their website in the about section or executive team. You can also Google the company and find the CEO. You should review their bio, news articles, and previous accomplishments

What should I look for in my research?

You want to look at the product or services to see if it is sustainable. You want to look at the CEO and management team. You want to see their track record to ensure they can manage the company to success and you want to make sure they have the funds to sustain so you want to look over their financials.

Chapter 8 Q & A

I did not sell my stock. Do I have to pay taxes on it?

No. You only pay taxes on stocks you sell. If you have not sold your stock you do not have realized profits.

Will I receive tax paperwork?

Yes. Your brokerage company will have your tax forms for you. They will email or mail it to you or you can simply pull them up in your account.

Should I save to purchase stock?

Yes, I would allocate a specific pot of money dedicated to stocks. This way you are not using the money you need for your daily living.

How can I control my FOMO?

Simply by doing your research. It's easy to get excited in the stock market. Just keep in mind your goal is profit and FOMO can cause you not to have a profit on your investment.

My stock has dropped, but I know it's a great company. What should I do?

If you know the company is great and you believe the drop is temporary I would buy more stock if you can and keep the stocks you have.

I hope that I have inspired you to consider investing. I have been on this journey for quite sometime and I must say it's been exciting and profitable. This book I provided some basic information about investing. There is so much more to learn and discover. This book was intended to open your mind up to the stock market. If you take the leap of investing I would encourage you to continue to research, learn and develop your investment technique.

Your journey to financial freedom will not happen overnight but if you do not start the journey will be longer than needed. Do not be afraid to try something new. As we said you don't need to be a Harvard graduate to invest in this market. All you need is time, patiences, basic math skills and a critical eye. Now is the time to think out the box and start investing.

I wish your luck and prosperity on your road to financial freedom.

Thank you for reading!!!

About the Author

Shylise M. Simpson

19

in

Shylise Simpson has over 19 years of professional business development and motivational experience. Ms. Simpson has worked her entire business career in the political, entertainment, and non-profit arena. She currently holds a Bachelor of Arts degree in Business Administration. Having a passion for the community Ms. Simpson worked passionately with the Community Coalition to eradicate social and economic injustices. Following her time at the Community Coalition, Ms. Simpson went on to become the assistant and scheduler to Assemblymember Karen Bass (currently Congress Woman).

Working for others in the business world in her early career, she was often challenged to correct specific issues and problems within the parent company, or often, with branches, subsidiaries, and partners. The rewards of these challenges and the successes that followed led to the passion for a transition to a full-time, independent small-business advisor, management consultant, and event planner.

Not to be confused with a "financial manager" Ms. Simpson works with all operational and personality and cultural issues within a company that impact profits, and more importantly, improved quality of life for owners and employees

Working as a business advisor, management consultant, and motivator to over 75 small business owners, Ms. Simpson has initiated and implemented successful changes in several areas; Such as raising over $150,000 through event strategizing and fundraising techniques; successfully received over $300,000 and grant funding for non-profit organizations; Strategize and implemented successful business plans increasing business revenue by 50%.

Ms. Simpson has enjoyed building and maintaining long-lasting relationships with many diverse clients. She has worked with over 15 different types of businesses and found that the basic principles she espouses pertain to all, and the major difference is how to implement the necessary changes with such a variety of personalities and company cultures, Ms. Simpson thrives on, and has a passion for these challenges.

She has learned from each company and each person she has worked with how to better help her next clients, learning what works best for most, and what does not work, and needs not to be repeated. Ms. Simpson has been described by Owners as being "street smart", "a person with uncommon perseverance", "having a unique ability to quickly implement realistic solutions", "people-oriented", "a team-builder", "having bold approaches to problems", "having the courage of telling owners 'as it is", and "professional at all times".

Thank you and keep me posted on your investment journey send email to shylise.simpson@gmail.com

www.ingramcontent.com/pod-product-compliance
Lightning Source LLC
Chambersburg PA
CBHW051455150726
48000CB00005B/2409